UNEVEN FROWN

UNEVEN FROWN

A Collection of Poems, Thoughts, and Musings

ANNA J. KIMBALL

Anna J. Kimball

CONTENTS

For Goose

The biggest heart this world has ever known,
and the sweetest soul I have ever loved.

Right Side

I stare at my young face in the mirror
reflecting the short time I've been here
only twenty-two years old
faint wrinkles beginning to sprout
devastated to notice
my frown lines between my brows
are so prominent
while my smile lines
are imperceptible
-born blue

I want to love you
I want it so desperately my lungs burn
the guilt I feel when you stare longingly
is terrible enough to make my guts churn
you are everything I could ever need and more
but it is his heart I will forever yearn

You always think, "If it happens to me, I'll put up a fight. I will scream, kick, and claw. I won't make it easy." Because that's what they tell you to do; that's what happens in the movies and TV shows like *Criminal Minds*. The victim always puts up a struggle against her attacker. But nobody prepares you for the fact that if it does happen, your mind might possibly cause the worst kind of betrayal you've ever experienced. Your mind might turn off completely, and you will lie there and allow it to happen to you. You will put up no fight; you will not scream, kick, or claw. You will not even cry. It will be quiet the entire time, besides the few whispered protests you make initially. Explaining you don't want to have sex, that you can't have sex with him because you have a boyfriend. But he will wipe away your tears, gently put his fingers to your lips, and tell you, "Everything is going to be okay." And you believe him because friends don't rape friends, so what's happening to you isn't rape at all.

The flowers are two weeks old today. They sit in the center of the kitchen table withered and brown. Drained of the beautiful bloom they once knew. The water in the vase has evaporated sending them into drought. All unrecognizable, save for a perfect white lily. I keep them here out of melancholy of the last act of kindness from you. The last gift you gave before destroying everything. I, like the lily, am clinging to the last bit of us I have left. A bandage covering all the blood and suffering from the last two years. I know eventually the lily will die and I will have to say goodbye to her like I said goodbye to you. For now, I will let the delusion live a little longer, and the flowers will stay.

-bloom amidst the rot

Fingertips graze over my cheeks brushing my tears
Fingertips placed on my lips shushing my fears
Fingertips loving, soft, and kind
Fingertips with something else on their mind
Fingertips slowly travel below my belt
Fingertips all too aware of the fate they've dealt
Fingertips full of want
Fingertips remain on my skin forever to haunt

I'm sorry for kissing you
for letting you believe I was yours
I've loved you in my own way
never letting myself fully shut the door

Now, you're in the aftermath, and your mind will continue to betray you for days, months, and years later. For the first few days, you don't even believe it happened. You wake up every morning feeling the way you did each day before. Nothing has changed. There was no traumatic event, and you don't tell anyone.

I catch myself crying often
thinking about your death
a world without you feels unbearable
so tonight I stroke your head
and watch your chest rise and fall
thanking the stars you're here another day
  -my truest love

he was the sun
the center of our solar system
people gravitated toward him like planets
the brightest star
when that light collapsed in on itself
we all stopped spinning
  -saddest death

grey skies were the home of my reveries
I found beauty in the way the earth
reflected my state of mind

Two weeks go by, and you're consumed with guilt. After all, you're convinced that you're this shitty person that cheated on their boyfriend and let another boy shove his penis in your mouth and inside you because you never said the word "stop."

you are always with me
gripping my wrist
until your knuckles are white
even when I don't want you
you are there
like a balloon tied to a child
by a strong steel string
floating above me forever
  -sadness

I grieve for the life that could have been
the wedding
the house
the kids
I grieve for who I used to be
the innocent
the optimist
the romantic
mostly I grieve for the man you were meant to be
the lover
the giver
the protector
  -you ruined us

terrified of:
terrified of hurting my flesh
terrified of leaving scars behind on an innocent
terrified of the monsters in my head
terrified of them procreating in my child's brain
terrified most of ruining them forever
  -motherhood

Months go by, and you're questioning why you keep having nightmares every night. And now you can't even kiss a boy in without feeling like you're on the verge of dying. And by the time you suddenly realize that you were indeed raped, it's too late. You've moved away to college, and the time to get a rape kit is long gone, and everyone knows you two were friends. Even though he's ruined your life, you feel guilty thinking about ruining his. And you're mad that you feel guilty because he didn't think about how raping you would change your life forever. But you know his mom and his brother; how could you let them look at him any differently? It doesn't matter anyway because you didn't even believe you were raped in the first place, so how could anyone believe you now? All the while, he is reaching out two times a week out of anxiety, asking you how you like Laramie and if you happen to remember that one night back in June. You say no every time because the thought of admitting it makes you want to vomit. And sometimes, when his name pops up on your phone, you do vomit. You become plagued with paranoia that he will find you and do it again. You get a new boyfriend, but sex is impossible, especially in the dark, because every single time, he turns into your rapist. His hands become the slightest bit too rough, and you're now sobbing uncontrollably because you're taken back to that night. He will turn on a lamp and look at you like you're crazy. And you try to explain, but it always ends with him becoming frustrated and asking if you could handle a handjob.

I am angry because as a child
I was told I was mature for my age
as if it were a compliment
and not a complete tragedy

"come back to me," he whispers seductively
shadows curling around the edges of my mind
too long I have kept away from his dark embrace
too long relishing in the light
he begs for my soul to be his again
to have complete control of me
for now I stand my ground
and refuse to let him have my hand
even though he is the most constant companion
and comfort I've ever had
  -depression

a sudden crack
a burst of pain
my vision goes black
crimson bloodstain

apologies repeated
with an abundance of kisses
my soul is depleted
along with all of my wishes

It's been an entire year, and you still haven't cried when you think about it because part of your mind still believes you don't remember it right and it never happened while the other part knows it happened, but you're not even able to say the word "rape" out loud. So, of course, you won't cry over something you can't say. So you begin telling people you were assaulted. Because 'assaulted' is a hell of a lot easier to say than rape. Each time you confide in a person and tell them your story, their first question is, "Did you report it?" Which makes you feel a gut-wrenching amount of shame as you shake your head silently. They try to hide their disappointment every time, but you know they think you're a coward. And you agree that you are a coward, and why didn't you report it as soon as it was over?

The little girl in me vanished that day; you took me to bed and decided I was yours for the night. Sometimes at two a.m. I hear her cries. I look for her hiding spot that must be deep in my soul. But all I find are ashes left behind of the girl I once knew. She fled my body the moment you put your hands on my breasts. I mourn her, wondering where she traveled to. I pray for her. I whisper to nature, asking if they've seen her. The world never answers me, but I know she's out there somewhere. Somewhere.

how am I supposed to have self-identity
when I have lived my whole life
for everyone else

I see you trying
your desperation to be wanted
your need to be needed
how you look at every face in the room
for validation after telling a joke
never wanting to be too much
or too little
trying to be just enough
  -I see you, I hear you, I want you

It takes years before you cry. Before you say the word rape. Before you learn, what happened to you was not your fault. Before you write about it.

when I have a child
I will know everything
their favorite saturday-morning-cereal
what position they sleep in
how they take their tea
where they part their hair
you don't even know my favorite color

I sit outside of your classroom
eyes swollen from silent sobs
needing you like a father
but not wanting to be a bother
looking toward the sky
begging for any greater being
to take away this grief
praying for you to tell me
"it'll be okay"
  -guilty

ink smears on my fingertips
as I write about all the ways
you've ruined my life

I hope I visit you in your nightmares
colorful visions of our torrid love affair
I hope my cries wake you from the dead of night
a piercing shrill sharp enough to bite
I hope you feel like you've seen a ghost
a silhouette of the one who loved you most
I hope the shame you feel is all-encompassing
preventing you from going back to slumbering

I dreamt about you
little button nose
darling green eyes
tiny hand wrapped around my index finger
soft brown curls on your head
you were mine and I was yours
   -waking up was brutal

I used to do everything for you
lived and breathed for your approval
I believed you did everything for me too
refusing to see our relationship as unusual

I miss the laughs we shared
how you would sing the entire drive to wyoming
you and me were the perfect pair
now I'm alone with the memories, forever roaming

you stare at me and for a moment
and I think you will notice
I got my crooked teeth finally fixed
we sit in silence a moment longer
before you say
"did I tell you I'm moving to Kentucky?"
you look down at your plate
and my heart breaks
you never notice anything about me
  -father

you shot me directly in the heart
and buried me in the backyard
departing from my corpse
leaving me the gifts
of a broken mind and a tattered soul
  -death by twenty

an angel kneels before me
in a velvet dress of emerald green
I am where you left me in the hotel hallway
mascara smudged from tears on downtown broadway
my life has become nothing but chaos and clatter
I've just lost the one thing that truly mattered
her soft hand reaches out and meets tender skin
she tells me quietly *you can do so much better than him*
　-christmas in nashville

I saw your mother at the supermarket today. Her basket brimmed with everyday essentials, eggs, bread, the mundane necessities of life. As she moved down the aisle, drawing closer to where I stood, our gazes locked. A polite smile graced her lips, the sort strangers give each other on a crowded sidewalk. In that moment, a wave of realization crashed over me like a wave of ice. She didn't recognize me. Dread settled in the pit of my stomach, heavy and suffocating.

I wish I'd never met you
spent years and tears on something untrue
drowning in self-pity and deprivation
the nurse hit the call button for resuscitation

you gallivanted ostentatiously around me
rubbing salt in the wound mercilessly
you drank away my memory at the small pub
while I lay on the tiled floor unable to get up

In the midst of the song's procession
I stand still teary eyed as
I watch my wife walking to me with her father in tow
in this moment joy floods my senses
she is the embodiment of radiance

for a fleeting moment the woman of my dreams
briefly turns into you
I take a shaky breath as my heart bottoms out
your youthful gaze locking with mine
I close my eyes and exhale

when I open them again it is my bride
my palms are sweating as I take her hands
I feel the weight of your memory
knowing you'll linger in the shadows
a haunting presence in the corners of my soul

I came across an old photo of your hands the other day. I knew they were yours from the size of your nailbeds and the scattered scars across your fingers. The hands that would throw me into the air as a little girl. "I would recognize these hands from anywhere," I thought to myself. As I stared at the picture, I was filled with deep despair. Would you recognize a photo of my hands? Would you see the bloodied cuticles and chipped polish and think *those are my daughter's hands?* Or would you not give it a second glance?

I wish your love for us
could echo the depths
of your love for her
   -we were here first

My entire existence has been molded to ensure the happiness of others, to be the most likable, the most agreeable, the most loveable. But how am I supposed to react when someone doesn't like me?

-thoughts that keep me awake

I wear your perfume on days
I know will be excruciating
that way you are with me
when I need you most

I drink red wine and weep
over a boy's soul taken
far too soon
   -will I ever get over this?

I nod as I let the words sink in
I know there is truth to them
yet within I feel like the epitome
of undesirability
  -the ugliest girl in the world

God must hate me
why else would he send me
through the burning embers of hell
if not to teach me a lesson?

I cried in a crowded *Applebees* today. My mother watched as the tears flowed freely down my cheeks. I had lost something that wasn't even mine. Caught up in fantasies about you and the beautiful life we would've had. I felt silly for crying over something that hadn't existed, but for two minutes it felt so real. In a quick bathroom trip, the life I had built in my head crumbled before the last brick was laid.

-grieving what never was

in this twisted labyrinth I've wandered long
seeking relief from wounds deep and strong
from counselors' chairs to mystic's art
I've searched for answers to soothe my devastated heart

like a bubble in my chest you continue to grow
cracked nails and torn cuticles to show
sleepless nights from your constant torment
you're with me no matter how often I repent
  -anxiety

I remember when the only monsters I feared were those who lingered under my bed. Now, I find myself glancing over my shoulder, wary of shadows that might hold the presence of men.

-he was my friend

I'm walking down the road as rain relentlessly falls
my shoes and hair are now drenched, soaked through
head bowed I watch raindrops splash on walls
a scent familiar, hitting with force anew
deja vu's grip unshakable, holds tight
I whip my head around seeking your face
everywhere I look in this dreary light
no one's there, just a hollow empty space
alone I stand amidst the chilling air
your absence cuts a knife within my chest
echoes of memories stark and bare
in this downpour I find no peace no rest
the rain persists a relentless embrace
in solitude I wander in this vast place

I miss my days as a girl
the days I would run free
not a care in the world

when being loud was tolerated
miss-matched clothing accepted
before learning of world hatred

I think of her all the time
her curly hair and crooked smile
sadly she is no longer mine

one foot in
one foot out
a family delighted in sin
another experiencing a love drought

two sides of the same coin
an interchangeable pain
a unique club impossible to join
shackle bound with an infinite chain

even after it all
if you were to call
I would wish you well
when I should scream go to hell

tears trail down my tired cheeks
all I've known is agony for weeks
I look to the sky and clasp my hands in a prayer
I just want to be good I plead to anyone up there
I sit quiet as I wait for a sound
any sign that someone might be around
the silence draws on no hint or clue
that a greater being can save me from my doom

hitting rock bottom is lovely
there's no where to go but up
from here

woke up feeling sick with dread
your face all over my dreams and skin
bitter taste in my mouth, wishing I were dead
returning to you would be my greatest sin

your beautiful bride lay in your bed
but I'm in your mind where I've always been
you can't swallow the guilt of how you watched as I bled
without me your life is gray-washed in chagrin

Left Side

I have an uneven frown
half of my soul is
queen of the dark
dweller of the somber, tragic castle
the other half
princess of the cosmos
tenant of the brilliant, euphoric sun
equal parts tormented and jubilant

your finger perfectly traces
the outline of the constellation
you stare at the sky dazzled by the stars
while I stare completely dazzled by you
    -I'll never view the big dipper the same

Perhaps it's the glass of wine I've had tonight. Or maybe it's my mind's way of finally admitting the feelings I've suppressed for so long. I'm not sure if it is because you are forbidden for me ever to touch, or because I have to be near you whenever you are in the room. The air around you acts as an atmosphere and never lets me drift too far away. How my heart stutters when you say my name and my breath catches when we accidentally touch—sleepless nights spent in my reveries of you declaring your adoration to me. Possibly, I am just a young girl in love with the idea of love, and this is all a very eloquent way of saying that I catch myself thinking about you when I shouldn't.

I twirl your curl around my finger
you are the most beautiful thing
that I have ever known
everything I love in this world
is alive in your soul

my love for you is so intoxicating
one kiss and suddenly I am the drunk girl
at the bar begging the bartender
not to cut her off

in my dreams we are friends again
your mom gives me hugs
and we hold hands as we laugh

I see the milky way
when your hands roam
freely on my skin
   -thank you for making love safe again

chameleon:
the ability to blend in any social setting
perfectly concealed from those who
are not trained to see when one does not belong

my black desolate soul turned to blush
the first time I heard your laugh

you taste so good
you whisper in between breaths
making out in your car
listening to *Cigarettes After Sex*

I fell in love before a boy's lips ever touched my own. As soon as I learned to read, my nose was constantly between the pages of a book. My youthful heart yearned to see the world from a different perspective. I went on many adventures and traveled to all seven continents before I could drive. I suffered through heart-shattering breakups before I ever had a boyfriend. I was a man, a queen, a cancer patient, a soldier, a widow, a witch, a homeless person, and much more. I have learned more about life from people who have never existed than I have in school. I have always found comfort in my literary heroes, and am grateful for the empathy I have learned from the pages I've read.

   -I really love to read

I was born with a pen between my fingers
writing about joy and pain and anything that lingers
my pen and paper gave me a purpose
after many years spent feeling worthless
creating a place for me to hide from this world
where I could truly flourish, my personality unfurled

I dream about leaving someday
sailing a boat to somewhere far away
a small place in Ireland where I can sit and read
distant from the ones full of selfishness and greed
only the soft and kind are allowed there
filtering out the loss and despair
life will be happy and life will be green
all the wretchedness will be wiped clean

I write about you
in the journal your father gave me

at sixteen entranced by you it seems
summer's grace young love's sweet schemes
falling fast like dawn's first hues
watching you go feeling unbearably blue

if you were to look up the
definition of a *good girl*
you will find a picture of my face
next to the description

we sway back and forth in silence
dancing in the small yellow kitchen
your touch the gift of Midas
gold glimmers leave me smitten
  -our tiny kingdom of joy

I've never had a muse
but if I did it would
surely be you

I dread that my heart will never again dance to the melody of love's song. Like a fragile rose denied the sun's warm touch, I'll linger in shadows, aching for the light of affection that once brightened my days.

-if you were to go

you were my life raft in the stormy sea
your sweet brown eyes a light guiding me
with your wide smile hope did arrive
that I would make it out alive

soaked in sunshine and drunk off of joy
swimming in circles around my favorite boy
the seltzers the salt water and the sweet dog
happiness surrounds us as a thick fog
if I could I would bottle this moment and keep it forever
this time with these people to visit whenever

I am drowning in a pool of desire
bones crackling in the heat of the fire

things that make me feel complete bliss:
snow on christmas morning
going through old photos
soft grass on bare feet
rain
making a baby laugh
making anybody laugh
hugging someone after not seeing them for a long time
puppy kisses
dancing with you
dinner by candlelight
drinking white wine with friends
writing a great verse

my hands are worn and rough as leather
a sign of the years of hard work and labor
your voice soft as the breath of a feather
a chance encounter through an unsuspecting neighbor

before you, my life was as harsh as this desert
barren and bleak no sign of intelligence
you cleared the dust away and created an oasis
now I am full of purpose and color

I often find myself in a paradoxical position: I feel both behind and ahead in life. While I have not yet married or started a family, my career is advancing, and I have the companionship of a loyal dog. I look to my left and see full-fledged families, and I look to my right and see peers who are still immersed in their studies. I feel overwhelming pressure to pick up the pace while simultaneously dreading growing up.

-twenties

I am in awe of the way you chase your dreams
despite being told you're not enough, you beam
you stand tall and resilient through every test
your determination shines, your unwavering zest
   -A

quiet giggles
glasses of wine
sharing secrets
painted nails
bounds of bliss
zero prejudice
crying together
wyd texts
chatting all night
  -female friendships

I've long known the embrace of man
of tough skin and strong hands
but I have a well of desire for more
for softness and a life not yet explored
long blonde hair shimmering in the sun
to touch your lips and become one
cross over the blurred lines
and act without thinking, just one time
  -Lola

I know what it feels like to have feelings so big you're unsure how to categorize them. I know what it feels like to have two separate families but feel like you don't belong in either one. It can feel like perpetually being on the outside, looking in. I know you want to take up the least space possible while being the best in the room. I know how hard you will try.

Family members will tell you they're disappointed in you, and friends will make you tiptoe in your own house. Loved ones will die, and you are going to make mistake after mistake after mistake. You will make yourself sick trying to look a certain way and jump through hoops to make people like you. You will try on personalities like they are different colored lipsticks. It is going to be exhausting, and eventually, you will burn yourself to ash, and there will be nothing left to give.

But the good news is once you've given every piece of yourself away, you may begin to rebuild it all exactly the way you want. The nights are long, and the scars run deep, but at twenty-three years old, you will finally be able to take a deep breath. No longer drowning under the expectations of others. Free to breathe and be. You will not be *good* or *bad*. You will just be.
   -letter to my younger self

ACKNOWLEDGEMENTS

This book has been a dream of mine for years. *Uneven Frown* is so special to me and those who helped make this dream a reality.

Cheyenne Hume, a fantastic friend, editor, and ball-of-sunshine wrapped into one. You helped my confidence in writing poetry soar. Your advice has helped shape this book more than you could know. Between our long chats discussing ideas, emails, and notes of your thoughts (also sorry about the depression), this book is just as much yours as it is mine. I will be grateful to you forever and ever.

To Makala Lybarger for the beautiful cover art. Thank you so much for your support and dedication. In fact, people judge books by their covers, and your art makes this one a very desirable read.

To Colt Klements, my high school English teacher. For always reading my stories outside of school and hyping me up even when my work was terrible. You made me fall in love with writing, and without your support, I wouldn't be here now. I'm more grateful than you know.

Hyleigh Gines for fueling me with wine and laughter

during this process. Our friendship is something I will never take for granted.

My sister Korinne and niece Arraya, thank you for your unwavering love. You both have been part of this journey since the very first poem. I love you.

To Danielle Lamb, for telling me I am good enough to write a book and always reminding me, "Fuck what everyone else thinks. " Thank you for all your help this last year.

To my girls, you know who you are. You women have shaped and impacted my life for the better. I am in constant awe of you all. Thank you for meeting me where I am and loving me despite it all.

To Haylen Cordova, my twin flame, best friend, sister, confidant, muse, and soulmate. I am the person I am today because of you. You have shown me colors I didn't even know existed. The joy you bring into my life is remarkable. Thank you for the beautiful interior art and your unshakeable loyalty. You are amazing.

To my mom, thank you for everything. Seriously... everything. I'm tremendously blessed to have you as a mom. I am a writer because of you. Thank you for your unconditional love and support.

Lastly to Goose, for being my life support during my darkest days and being the goodest boy. This book is for you.

Anna J. Kimball is a writer currently residing in Wyoming. When she is not writing, she is playing with her dog or crying to Taylor Swift songs.